Guidelines for developing national drug policies

WORLD HEALTH ORGANIZATION
GENEVA
1988

In order to ensure prompt distribution, these guidelines have not received such detailed editorial revision as most other WHO publications.

ISBN 92 4 154230 6

The designations employed and the presentation of the material in this publication do not imply the expression of any opinion whatsoever on the part of the Secretariat of the World Health Organization concerning the legal status of any country, territory, city or area or of its authorities, or concerning the delimitation of its frontiers or boundaries.

The mention of specific companies or of certain manufacturers' products does not imply that they are endorsed or recommended by the World Health Organization in preference to others of a similar nature that are not mentioned. Errors and omissions excepted, the names of proprietary products are distinguished by initial capital letters.

PRINTED IN SWITZERLAND

88/7551–IAM–4000

Contents

Preface

During a WHO Conference of Experts on the Rational Use of Drugs, held in Nairobi in November 1985, the World Health Organization was requested to convene a group of experts to prepare guidelines for establishing national drug policies. This request was repeated by the Thirty-ninth World Health Assembly in 1986 in resolution WHA39.27 on the rational use of drugs, endorsing WHO's revised drug strategy.

As a consequence, a Working Group of Experts met in Geneva from 16 to 20 March 1987 to draft guidelines for national drug policies.[1] (A list of participants is given in Annex 1.) The guidelines were later reviewed by the WHO Executive Board *Ad Hoc* Committee on Drug Policies, which met in Geneva on 9–10 January 1988 (see list of participants in Annex 2). This publication incorporates amendments and changes made by the *Ad Hoc* Committee.

The goal of a drug policy is to develop, within the resources of a country, the potential that drugs have to control common diseases and alleviate suffering. While these guidelines are intended for use in any country, they have been framed specifically to help those that are just starting to formulate a national drug policy. In reality, countries are at different stages of development and may already have various policies and methods for their implementation. The guidelines will therefore need to be adapted in the light of local needs, the type of economy, and other circumstances. The guidelines incorporate the concept of essential drugs[2] but allow for economic, social, and other differences among countries.

---

[1] In these guidelines, the term "drug" refers to pharmaceutical preparations used for medicinal purposes.

[2] The term "essential drugs" refers to drugs that are of the "utmost importance, and are basic, indispensable and necessary for the health needs of the population" (WHO Technical Report Series, No. 615, 1977, p. 9). For a glossary of other terms used in this report, see Annex 3.

Introduction

The goal of health for all by the year 2000 has been accepted by most countries. To achieve it, a strategy needs to be framed and incorporated in a written policy. Such a strategy must include a satisfactory health care system. The prevention and treatment of disease require an adequate health care delivery infrastructure and appropriate education, and high priority must be given to ensuring adequate sanitation, safe water supplies, and proper nutrition. In addition, drugs and vaccines have the potential to confer enormous health benefits on a large number of people.

Many countries have frequently lacked adequate supplies of drugs. The reasons for this are complex and are not only the result of financial and budgetary constraints, but also reflect the attitude and behaviour of the government, prescribers, dispensers, consumers, and the drug industry. To ensure an adequate supply of safe and effective drugs of good quality, every country should have a national drug policy as an integral part of its health policy. Appropriate legislation and regulations will be needed to help implement such a policy.

A vital requirement is that governments should exert the political will necessary to formulate and implement a drug policy. Lack of political will, even more than lack of resources, has been a decisive factor in the failure of some countries to ensure adequate provision of drugs and vaccines.

The minister of health is the most appropriate person to take the lead in developing a national drug policy. However, other government officials will need to participate in its development, since its success will depend on the interest and wholehearted endorsement of government officials at the highest levels with areas of responsibility that affect implementation of the policy. Of particular importance are the officials responsible for planning, finance, education, industry, and commerce, since decisions regarding import quotas, trade barriers, transfer pricing, foreign exchange allocations, and tariffs may all have significant effects on drug procurement, manufacturing, and use. A national drug policy should, therefore, provide mechanisms whereby the health sector can influence and be actively involved in decision-making in other sectors.

The first step in establishing a national drug policy is to prepare a detailed quantitative and qualitative analysis of the health resources (manpower, financial, physical) and health requirements of the country. This analysis should not only cover the national situation but also take into account the resources and other benefits that may accrue from regional and international cooperation. The long-term consequences of short-term benefits and any possible disadvantages must also be carefully considered.

The following subdivisions of each area of analysis may be suggested:

National

(1) Levels of health care – primary, secondary, tertiary, public and private.

(2) Health subsectors – universities, hospitals, professional associations, pharmaceutical manufacturers and distributors.

(3) Ministries and government bodies – health, education, trade and industry, judiciary, legislature, finance and planning.

International

Intercountry or regional cooperation (e.g., Caribbean Community (CARICOM), Association of South East Asian Nations (ASEAN), Andean Pact) is one means of efficiently utilizing scarce resources, particularly for the production and/or procurement of pharmaceuticals.

All available data should be sought on the following:

— the incidence and prevalence of disease, demographic data;
— current and past use of pharmaceutical products (generic and branded), including consumption and prescribing patterns;
— current and past health expenditure, in the public and private sectors and in major health subsectors;
— existing health and drug legislation and regulations, professional codes;
— sources of raw materials, pharmaceutical products, manufacturers, distributors (national, regional, international);
— available resources – financial (including foreign exchange), manpower, physical, education.

Once the data are available, the implications should be discussed in an appropriate forum with all the interested parties, including professional groups, health workers, consumers, health teaching staff, and pharmaceutical manufacturers. Full consideration should be given to the concerns and advice of all to ensure that the policy takes into account the expressed needs of the interested parties and thus encourages their participation in its implementation.

1. Components of a drug policy

Legislation and regulation

Legislation and regulation constitute important elements in any drug policy. The legal framework must take into account not only policy objectives but also the administrative, social, and health infrastructure, the available manpower, and other resources. The formulation of a drug policy should be followed immediately by enactment of appropriate legislation and introduction of regulations to provide a legal basis and make the policy enforceable.

A law serves the primary function of distinguishing between what is permissible and what is not. A drugs act, for instance, may stipulate who can import or manufacture drugs or who can prescribe certain categories of drugs. Various authorities are needed to carry out a drug policy; their powers, duties, and responsibilities should be clearly defined in the legislation.

Drug legislation and regulation must address the rights and responsibilities of the different parties concerned with drugs and pharmaceutical products, including medical practitioners, pharmacists, importers, manufacturers, and distributors. These parties play different roles in ensuring that the needs of consumers are met. The legislation must itself establish the qualifications required for those entitled to handle drugs or it must state who has the authority to do so.

Legislation plays an important role in ensuring that pharmaceutical products are of acceptable quality, safety, and efficacy. It must also regulate their availability and distribution.

Legislation must also specify the sanctions that will apply in the event of failure to conform with any provisions of an act. Sanctions must be enforced if the policy is to function effectively.

Several legislative models and structures have been devised for the regulation of drugs (*1*). The circumstances of the country will determine the model or structure selected, but the basic elements listed below represent the minimum framework. Legislation and regulation should cover both the public and the private sector.

The basic elements are as follows:

(*a*) *General provisions*: title, purposes, extent, application.

(*b*) *Specific provisions*: control of the import, export, and manufacture of drugs and of distribution, supply, storage, and sale.

(*c*) *Other provisions*: authority for the regulation of labelling, information and advertising, drug registration, scheduling of controlled substances, imposition of fees, and price controls.

(*d*) *Drug control administration*: organization and function, mechanism of appeals against decisions.

(*e*) *Prohibitions, offences, penalties and legal procedures.*

(*f*) *Assignment of powers to make rules and regulations.*

(*g*) *Repeals of existing laws in conflict with the Act and transitional provisions.*

(*h*) *Exemptions from the provisions of the law.*

These elements are sufficiently comprehensive and varied in scope to meet most of the objectives of a national drug policy. Some developing countries may not need all of them in the initial stages of implementation of a national drug policy. For instance, provisions covering manufacture would not be relevant in a country that has no immediate plans to engage in domestic production.

After a law has been enacted, the appropriate authority should draw up the regulations governing the standards and procedures for carrying out the provisions of the law. These regulations form the second stage of legislative procedures and are specifically designed to provide the legal machinery to achieve the administrative and technical goals.

Regulatory control

Drug control administration[1]

A drug control administration should be established and its duties and powers defined in law. In some countries the functions of such an administration or regulatory authority are financed through the imposition of fees for registration or licensing of pharmaceutical products and the licensing of premises. Its functions should cover such aspects of drug regulatory control as evaluation, registration or licensing, review and renewal, quality control, and inspection. Another responsibility is the control of manufacturing standards and practices, drug imports, exports, distribution, labelling, pricing, information dissemination, sales promotion, and advertising. The drug control administration should be responsible for determining the conditions on which marketing approval is granted, for establishing the type of drug product information to be provided, and for monitoring its content.

[1] This topic was discussed in detail at a consultation on guiding principles for small national drug regulatory authorities, held in Geneva from 1 to 6 November 1987. For more information, write to: Pharmaceuticals, World Health Organization, 1211 Geneva 27, Switzerland.

The staff should be adequately trained, have clearly defined functions and powers, and be entrusted with responsibility for inspection of premises, processes, and records in order to ensure compliance with the law. If required, the control administration should be able to call on outside experts or set up advisory committees to deal with, for example, specific questions relating to drug approval and control.

Drug registration and licensing

The process for approval of pharmaceutical products, known as "registration" or "licensing" in some countries, involves a series of different but complementary procedures. In a comprehensive drug registration system, adequate data on pharmaceutical, pharmacological, toxicological, therapeutic and clinical investigations must be available, and the personnel must have the ability to analyse the data. Documentation on these subjects is now very extensive because of advances in medical and pharmaceutical knowledge and stricter requirements for safety and efficacy. Countries that do not have the professional staff to evaluate and handle such documentation fully may wish to seek technical advice from WHO and/or from other countries with more advanced regulatory agencies. They may also wish to take account of regulatory decisions made in other countries. The authorities in some countries publish summary assessments of specific drugs and/or brief explanations of their reasons for rejecting applications for pharmaceutical product approval.

A registration authority may evolve in stages, by establishing increasing levels of control (*2*):

(*a*) *Notification procedure*. This involves obtaining information on all pharmaceutical products offered for sale in the country. The amount of information requested in a notification may vary. It may initially be restricted to the names of the pharmaceutical product and of the manufacturer. It may then be expanded to require notification of the nonproprietary names for active substances, the composition (including inactive ingredients), the pharmacological action, and the therapeutic classification.

(*b*) *Authorization procedure*. Such a procedure is designed to ensure that pharmaceutical products are authorized before they can be marketed in the country. The procedure may vary in its stringency but almost always incorporates some element of inspection of the manufacturer's facilities and the verification of product quality.

(*c*) *Registration or licensing procedure*. This comprises detailed evaluation of data submitted in support of the safety, efficacy, and quality of a pharmaceutical product; it also determines the indications for its use. The procedure includes an assessment both of the pharmaceutical product and of manufacturing procedures and facilities.

Cost and price

Some countries may wish to fix prices to the consumer. Such prices are generally determined either by calculations of cost or by the market situation.

When the prices of drugs are determined by *cost calculation*, the following are usually taken into account:

(*a*) the cost of *production*, including the production of raw materials, the formulation, packaging, quality assurance, marketing (comprising advertising and direct and indirect sales promotion), general administration, and returns on investment;

(*b*) the cost of *discovery*, research and development (including royalties for patents and know-how);

(*c*) the cost of *distribution*, including storage, transportation, sales promotion, client services, and general administration;

(*d*) the cost of *dispensing*, including technical, administrative, and storage expenses and miscellaneous expenses for consumer services.

A variable amount of profit and tax is added to these costs.

The main components of the above costs can be determined as fixed amounts or within acceptable limits as a percentage of the price. The most difficult components to evaluate in determining drug prices, however, are the production costs of intermediate and raw materials, which are generally known only to the producers.

The determination of drug prices needs to take into account:

— whether finished pharmaceutical products are imported;
— whether finished pharmaceutical products are produced locally;
— whether intermediate and/or raw materials are imported for local formulation.

Some countries may need to consider a variety of price control mechanisms, with a view to providing drugs within their financial resources and those of consumers.

Control of drug prices is practised in some countries with varying success. One approach is to develop regulations setting maximum drug prices. Another is to place drugs within the framework of general price regulation. A third is to make the price of a drug part of the registration requirement, taking into account, for example, the therapeutic importance of the drug, the price of equivalent preparations in the country, and the price of the same preparation in other countries. In some countries, sale prices are controlled by regulations governing social welfare reimbursement.

An important factor in considering controlling the price of drugs is the social and political orientation of the country; this will also influence the decision as to whether control should apply to the public sector only or also include the private sector. In some cases, control might be exercised over essential drugs only.

Prices vary from one country to another for reasons that sometimes make realistic comparisons difficult. A better appreciation of the circumstances in which drugs are supplied and improved data on cost factors related to, for example, the costs of raw materials, research and development, manufacturing and promotion, would make realistic comparisons more feasible.

Regulations on prescribing and dispensing at different levels of the health care system

As part of a national drug policy and to meet the objective of health for all by the year 2000, it is necessary to formulate and/or review legislation, rules, regulations, and professional codes that relate to the prescribing and dispensing of drugs. The development of primary health care in many countries requires that special attention be given to the role of village health workers in prescribing and dispensing.

The gap between manpower needs and availability makes it necessary to allow for some degree of flexibility in legislation and codes without compromising either the quality of health care or the objective of a safe and rational use of drugs. Countries may stipulate the drugs permitted to be prescribed at different levels of the health care system, according to the availability and competence of health personnel.

Choice of drugs and pharmaceutical products

Approval of pharmaceutical products

Safety, quality, and efficacy should be prerequisites for the approval for sale of a pharmaceutical product.

Number of drugs

There are arguments for and against limiting the number of drugs and pharmaceutical products. For various reasons some regulatory agencies, prepaid insurance systems, and hospitals limit the number of drugs that can be prescribed. A decision to limit the number of active substances and pharmaceutical products requires a balance to be found between several, sometimes conflicting, objectives.

The most important of these objectives is to establish a drug supply system that satisfies the health needs of the community and at the same time can respond to the health needs of the individual. Whatever the extent of limitation of the number of drugs, provision should be made to supply any approved pharmaceutical product excluded from the limited list to meet exceptional medical needs.

The number of drugs and pharmaceutical products selected will be influenced by the need to maintain a drug supply system of appropriate and manageable size in terms of the human and financial resources needed to monitor and control its operations effectively.

Selection of essential drugs

The selection of essential drugs to meet the health needs of the population is an important part of a national drug policy. It provides a rational basis not only for drug procurement at the national level but also for establishing and meeting drug requirements at different levels within the health care system.

As a first step, a process should be established for selecting the drugs to be included in the essential drugs list. Commonly a committee is set up which includes experts in clinical medicine, pharmacology, pharmacy and, where appropriate, nursing. In addition, in recognition of the fact that the success of any national drug policy depends on its general acceptance, mechanisms should be established for consultation with interested parties, including representatives of professional bodies, pharmaceutical manufacturers, and consumer and patient organizations. While such formal and informal consultation with representative interests is needed to ensure that the selection of drugs reflects broad policy objectives, the process of drug selection by the experts should be carried out independently.

The type and number of essential drugs selected will depend on the circumstances in which the drugs will be used, but the selection should be based on the essential drugs concept and in particular on the following criteria:

(*1*) Drug selection should be based on evaluations of benefit and safety obtained in controlled clinical trials and/or epidemiological studies; if necessary, reference may be made to regulatory authorities who have already taken decisions based on clinical trials. Guidelines for such trials have been set forth in the report of a WHO Scientific Group (*3*).

(*2*) Drugs should be selected by their international nonproprietary (generic) name (*4*). If necessary, a cross-index of nonproprietary and proprietary names should be supplied to prescribers and dispensers.

(*3*) Regulations should be formulated to ensure that the selected pharmaceutical products meet adequate quality control standards, including stability and, when necessary, bioavailability. Suppliers should provide documentation of the drug's compliance with the requested specifications. This is especially important where national resources are not available for this type of control.

(*4*) Cost represents a major criterion in selection. In comparing the costs of different drugs the following elements should be taken into account:

— the cost of the treatment regimen rather than the cost of the dosage form;
— the cost of treatment in relation to the savings made by, for example, reduction in the need for surgery or hospitalization;
— different rates of success of treatment achieved, as a result of improved patient compliance;
— reduced loss or waste achieved by using more stable products.

(*5*) The appropriate health authorities should decide on both the level of care and the qualifications of health workers required for prescribing one or more drugs in specific therapeutic categories. Consideration should also be given to the competence of such personnel to make a correct diagnosis. While in some cases health workers with higher training may be needed to diagnose and initiate treatment, it should be recognized that personnel with less training may be able to supervise maintenance therapy.

(*6*) The prevalence of particular diseases may in some cases require the use of one kind of drug rather than another. For example, malnutrition or liver disease may alter the absorption, distribution, metabolism, or excretion of some drugs.

(*7*) When several drugs are available with the same indication, or when two or more drugs are therapeutically equivalent, the aim should be to select the pharmaceutical product and dosage form that provide the most favourable benefit/risk ratio. Preference should be given to:

— the drugs that have been most thoroughly investigated;
— the drugs with the most favourable pharmacokinetic properties, e.g., those that improve compliance or minimize risk in various pathophysiological states;
— the drugs, pharmaceutical products, and dosage forms with the greatest stability or for which appropriate storage facilities exist.

In addition, preference should be given to drugs and dosage forms for which reliable local manufacturing facilities exist.

(*8*) Fixed-ratio combinations are usually only acceptable if one or more of the following criteria are met:

— the clinical condition justifies the use of more than one drug;
— the therapeutic effect of the combination is greater than the sum of the effects of each drug;
— the cost of the combination product is less than the total cost of the individual products;
— sufficient combinations are provided to allow adjustment of dosage to meet the needs of the majority of the population;
— compliance is improved.

(*9*) New drugs should be introduced into an essential drugs list only if they offer distinct advantages over drugs selected previously. If new information on drugs already in the list shows that they no longer have a favourable benefit/risk ratio, they should be deleted and replaced by safer drugs. It should be remembered that, for the treatment of certain conditions, non-pharmacological forms of therapy or no therapy at all may be preferable.

(*10*) The essential drugs list should be updated at least every second year and more often if necessary. Revision is likely to be needed because of advances in drug therapy and in order to meet the needs of practice in the light of clinical experience.

Traditional drugs

In many countries experience has been accumulated in the use of locally available drugs of natural origin, mainly medicinal plants, and some of them have been used effectively. These drugs, however, are not necessarily safe simply because they are natural; some have given rise to serious adverse reactions and some contain chemicals that may produce long-term effects such as carcinogenicity and hepatotoxicity. A number of traditional drugs could, however, be advantageously used in organized health care. Symptomatic treatment is frequently required in primary health care and in these cases the use of traditional drugs may often be medically and economically justified. Some countries may therefore wish to include traditional drugs in their national drug policy. It is important to evaluate the use of traditional drugs and simultaneously strengthen explorative and developmental research in traditional medicine. WHO can facilitate information exchange in this area and assist countries to strengthen their exploratory, developmental and evaluative research. When introducing traditional drugs into organized health care, countries should:
— identify the health conditions that can be effectively treated by traditional medicine, taking into consideration the pathophysiological and psychosomatic aspects of their symptoms;
— develop appropriate methodology and technology for the identification, production and development of traditional medicines to enhance their medical, economic and sociocultural benefits and acceptance;

- undertake scientific studies to evaluate the clinical efficacy and safety of the drugs, as well as chemical and biological studies to identify and isolate active substances in them that could be introduced into modern medicine;
- encourage patients, health workers, pharmacists, and doctors to notify adverse reactions, especially when herbal remedies are used in large amounts for prolonged periods.

The possibility of carcinogenic, mutagenic, and hepatotoxic effects should be investigated in countries where traditional drugs are widely used.

Supply

Drugs and/or pharmaceutical products are either imported or locally manufactured, or both.

Procurement

As pharmaceuticals represent an important part of public purchasing and are among the commodities most needed by a country, it is essential, particularly when economic resources are limited, that the government or public agencies should establish a system of procurement from multiple sources of supply, domestic or international. Substantial public savings can accrue from effective procurement. If the necessary marketing intelligence and a system of quality assurance are available, a relatively small qualified staff is required. Potential conflicts of interest are avoided if drug control and drug procurement functions remain administratively independent of each other.

Marketing intelligence is of enormous benefit for drug procurement and strengthens the country's bargaining power. It can be obtained through continuous survey and analysis of:

- producers, their manufacturing practices, and scale of production;
- price trends, with early detection of speculation and other influences on the market;
- the reliability of quality assurance, e.g., through batch certificates and control;
- information on new drugs, especially their registration status in the country of origin and elsewhere;
- information on product interchangeability, taking into consideration bioavailability and therapeutic equivalence.

In several developing countries a well organized procurement system, based on worldwide tender, has been established as one of the major activities of the ministry of health. The system includes facilities for storage (including a cold room), packing, repackaging, transport, basic quality control, and often production of some dosage forms, e.g., powders, ointments, solutions, and elixirs. The administration of such a system requires the technical and financial expertise that is provided by professionals such as pharmacists and accounting and statistical staff. Usually the procurement agency obtains not only pharmaceutical products and vaccines but also other medical equipment and materials.

Procurement procedures are based on tenders and, for specific bulk drugs and/or pharmaceutical products, on price negotiation under the responsibility of an independent committee of officials from several ministries – health, trade, and finance, including customs. Special allocations of foreign currency and exemptions from customs duty and tax are matters of considerable importance in the establishment of a procurement agency.

The first step in the procurement process is to prepare estimates of the types and quantities of pharmaceutical products that will be required annually, biannually, or quarterly to satisfy the needs of the health services. Ideally, estimates of types and quantities should be based on up-to-date health information and should take into consideration the available health budget allocations. In many developing countries these requirements are difficult to meet in the initial phase owing to incomplete or unreliable information regarding disease patterns; in practice, therefore, the estimates are usually based on past drug use, and may be re-evaluated and revised through inventory control and utilization surveys. A practical manual[1] containing methodologies for estimating drug requirements is available from the WHO Action Programme on Essential Drugs. These methodologies have proved helpful in achieving a more systematic approach to estimating drug requirements. Estimates are easier to obtain in specific disease control campaigns.

In order to keep the price of drugs low, products can be bought in bulk and repackaged in the country with standardized packing and labelling; the need for a clear distinction between different pharmaceutical products and their strengths should be kept in mind. For this purpose the procurement agency will require specialized technical staff for packing, stock-keeping, and quality control, and premises for storage and packing; this will increase the administrative costs.

The unit price of bulk drugs and/or pharmaceutical products can be considerably reduced by ordering large quantities. Tenders should therefore be requested annually, or at long intervals, for products that have a

---

[1] *Estimating drug requirements: a practical manual.* Unpublished WHO document, WHO/DAP/88.2. Available on request from: Action Programme on Essential Drugs, World Health Organization, 1211 Geneva 27, Switzerland.

long shelf-life and stable international prices. The procurement of patented products, or products produced by a few manufacturers, requires negotiation of price. Here market intelligence is of great importance.

Local production

There are three main types of pharmaceutical production:

— production of raw materials and intermediates;

— production of finished dosage forms from half-finished intermediates and raw materials (formulation);

— packaging of finished products or repackaging of bulk finished products.

The practicability of building up, step by step, a viable pharmaceutical production industry, with the aim of achieving self-reliance in pharmaceutical supplies, depends on many factors. These include: (*a*) population size and per capita income; (*b*) the available technical manpower and supporting infrastructure; (*c*) the geographical and climatic conditions; (*d*) water and energy supplies; and (*e*) the distribution network.

These are often major limiting factors. In many cases, it is not possible to produce economically all the pharmaceutical products needed in one country. Ideally, therefore, cooperation between countries is desirable. Some countries may wish to consider participating in regional arrangements with neighbours so as to achieve economies of scale and greater cost-effectiveness. For the long term, countries should strive to acquire at least the capacity to manufacture dosage forms with a view to preventing shortages due to unforeseen political or economic events and to making themselves as self-sufficient as possible. Before deciding to establish factories to produce finished dosage forms, long-term planning is required, taking into account the health needs of the population and the available financial and technical resources. The decision as to whether the essential drugs are to be produced by a government factory under the responsibility of the ministry of health or the ministry of industry or by private industry, from which requirements can be obtained at reasonable price, is one that depends on local conditions and the sociopolitical structure of the country. When local production of essential drugs is to be established it is important to ensure that the products meet appropriate standards of quality.

Objective feasibility studies are needed before local production can be undertaken. These should take into account such factors as:

— the size of the domestic market, its purchasing power, and the possibilities for the export of drugs to neighbouring or other countries. The assessment should include not only the size of the export market but the existence of similar production units elsewhere and the extent to which their capacity is utilized;

— the true foreign exchange costs, including hidden costs. This will include costs of raw materials, packaging, machinery and spare parts, repair services, other technical assistance, technology and licences, quality control equipment and services, the distribution network, advertising and promotion costs, electricity production and water purification;
— the effects on employment, the extent to which the highly skilled personnel needed are available locally, and how many unskilled workers will be employed.

In undertaking market analyses and other financial studies, particular attention must be paid to the prices of products with which locally produced drugs will compete. In some cases the prices of generic products in international trade may be lower than those of locally produced drugs.

Some countries may feel that one or more manufacturing plants will solve their import problems, reduce foreign exchange needs, provide employment, and contribute to an improvement in the balance of external trade through exports. Developing countries interested in undertaking local production should, however, take into account the following considerations:
— Command of the appropriate technology is a critical factor, but managerial maturity and skills are just as important.
— The capacity of the local market to absorb local production is often overestimated. The public sector of the local market may operate on a strictly limited budget.
— Exports to neighbouring or other countries can only be achieved if there is sufficient demand and if good quality drugs can be supplied at favourable prices.
— Local production should be aimed initially at the large-scale supply of essential drugs for primary health care.

Some local production may be desirable in every country. Any decision to proceed to the production of intermediates and raw materials must take into account the high technology required and the necessary presence of other related industries, such as the petrochemical industry, which are essential to such production.

Some categories of drugs or drug products, such as ointments, infusion fluids, and water for injection or irrigation, may be more suitable for local production. Materials for these products are generally available locally.

Vaccines need special consideration. Before a decision is made to produce vaccines, it is necessary to consider such factors as the rapid progress of biotechnology and the availability on the world market of vaccines of high quality and low price.

Distribution and storage

Distribution is a key factor in the pharmaceutical supply system. It is necessary to devise and implement a system that reaches the majority of the population, especially in the remote areas of the country. Such a system is often best based on a combination of private and public sector initiative. Drug manufacturers, wholesalers, and retailers can apply their entrepreneurial experience and skill to expanding distribution and bringing about greater efficiency.

The aim of a drug distribution policy is to ensure that the right drugs are always available to those in the population who need them. Drug distribution is too often considered in terms of storage and transportation by independent organizations or agencies responsible primarily for procurement and/or production. This helps produce an uncoordinated pharmaceutical supply system.

In distribution and storage, as elsewhere in the pharmaceutical supply system, the professional skills of pharmacists are vital.

The following are examples of distribution patterns:

(a) State monopoly → subdepots → pharmacies (retailers) → patients/consumers
subdepots ⇢ health institutions → patients

(b) Central procurement agency:
private sector store → wholesalers → pharmacies (retailers) → patients/consumers
public sector store → district stores → health institutions → patients

(c) Government: ministry of health → public sector → health institutions → patients
other ministries (e.g., trade, social security) → medical stores → pharmacies (retailers) → patients/consumers

(d) Private wholesalers → pharmacies (retailers) → patients/consumers
Private wholesalers ⇢ health institutions → patients

When planning or reorganizing a distribution system that includes central, intermediate, and peripheral storage facilities, the following needs should be considered:

— adequate storage facilities;
— adequate inventory control, including security;
— sufficient and appropriate transportation facilities and maintenance service;
— packaging material – standardization and labelling;
— quality surveillance;
— education and regular training of staff;
— a management information system;
— drug utilization surveys.

The major requirement in establishing a successful distribution system is proper education and training of the personnel involved, such as pharmacists, dispensers, administrative staff, inspectors, accountants, storekeepers, packers and transporters. Education and training can help prevent wastage and leakage of valuable drugs during distribution and improve the utilization of drugs for health care. Periodic seminars, workshops, and meetings on drug management (including information recording and analysis) are key factors in improving drug distribution.

Quality assurance of drug substances and products

Quality assurance is a system for monitoring the entire process from the acquisition of a pharmaceutical raw material to its conversion into a finished product made available to the consumer. Its purpose is to ensure that the user receives a product that meets all established specifications and standards.

The pharmaceutical supply system should aim to ensure the quality of all drug products. This will involve a series of complex operations, with checks, tests, and inspections carried out at all levels.

The minimum acceptable quality for drug substances and products should be the same in each country.

Elements of a drug quality assurance system

A quality assurance system has three basic facets: legal, regulatory, and technical.

(*a*) *Legal base*
The enabling legislation should provide the necessary authority for the development of specific regulations relating to quality assurance and assessment during the manufacture, importation, and distribution of drug substances and products.

(*b*) *Regulatory elements*
Regulatory elements should include a central administrative body, provision for inspection and recall (including emergency recall), and drug quality control laboratories.

(*c*) *Technical elements*
The technical elements of a quality assurance system should include quality specifications, basic tests, and requirements for good manufacturing practices.

WHO Certification Scheme on the Quality of Pharmaceutical Products Moving in International Commerce

The WHO Certification Scheme on the Quality of Pharmaceutical Products Moving in International Commerce is of especial potential value for countries with limited resources for drug control. Under the Certification Scheme, the exporting country must certify that the drug is registered and permitted to be sold in that country. If it is not, the reasons must be stated. The competent authority of the exporting country must also certify that the manufacturer's facilities are inspected regularly and that they comply with WHO standards of good practices in manufacture and quality control.

The WHO Certification Scheme is currently under review, since it is incomplete and does not deal with the basis for approval or the indications for which the product has been approved. Nor is there any provision for the certification of raw materials in the Scheme. Some governments, however, are prepared to give this information on request.

Despite the need for improvement, the WHO Certification Scheme is generally considered superior to free sales certificates[1] for finished products and should ultimately replace them. Until such time as the Scheme covers raw materials, however, free sales certificates for them serve a purpose.

---

[1] A free sales certificate certifies only that a pharmaceutical product is for sale in the exporting country. The WHO Certification Scheme, however, certifies that "the manufacturing plant in which the product is produced is subject to inspections at suitable intervals to show that the manufacturer conforms to requirements for good practices in manufacture and quality control, as recommended by the World Health Organization, in respect of products to be sold or distributed within the country of origin or to be exported" (*5*).

The WHO Certification Scheme cannot take the place of licensing and registration systems. It is intended to strengthen such systems, not replace them, and national quality control and assurance systems are still necessary.

Good practices in the manufacture and quality control of drugs

Overall quality control in the manufacture of drugs is essential to ensure that the consumer receives drugs of a high standard.

At the Twenty-eighth World Health Assembly in 1975, the revised text of *Good practices in the manufacture and quality control of drugs* was adopted (*5*). This text contains general guidelines covering the following areas:

Personnel.

Premises.

Equipment.

Sanitation.

Starting materials.

Manufacturing operations.

Labelling and packaging.

The quality control system.

Self-inspection.

Distribution records.

Complaints and reports of adverse reactions.

Quality control laboratories

Each country should establish a quality control laboratory as part of its national regulatory authority (*6*). The types and levels of checks, tests, and inspections made will depend on the manpower and financial resources of the country.

Stability of drug substances and products

Stability studies should cover all pharmaceutical substances, not just a few critical ones such as biological products; the stability of all drug substances and products under extreme tropical conditions is equally important.

It is expected that accelerated stability studies, coordinated by WHO, will shortly be extended to cover dosage forms. Their validity will need to be established by field studies in tropical countries with extreme climatic conditions.

Manpower aspects and development needs

Appropriately trained technical, administrative and health care personnel are needed to organize and operate the different elements of a drug policy. An analysis of staffing needs should be carried out and arrangements made for the training and continuing education of both managerial and technical personnel. Curricula for the training of pharmacists, physicians, and other health personnel should be drawn up so as to fulfil the needs of the activities under the drug policy. Particular emphasis should be placed on training in pharmacy, drug management, and clinical pharmacology. Pharmacists are required not only in hospitals and retail pharmacies but also for quality assurance, legislative, regulatory, and registration functions, drug control, quality control laboratories, drug manufacturing units, and drug supply and management (at the primary health care level also). Clinical pharmacologists are required to assist in drug evaluation and training in the rational use of drugs at all levels of health care.

Appropriately trained personnel should be employed to carry out quality assurance activities at all levels. Collaboration between WHO and the International Federation of Pharmaceutical Manufacturers' Associations (IFPMA) and the World Federation of Proprietary Medicines Manufacturers (WFPMM) on technical matters and training benefits countries in need of training for personnel in quality assurance. Through this collaboration, training in drug quality control and good manufacturing practices is offered to nationals of developing countries working in government drug control laboratories, in pharmaceutical inspection services, or in other departments of the health ministry concerned with drug control.

Long-term plans for manpower development are essential to ensure a balance between training activities and manpower needs. Career planning is important in helping to recruit personnel into government service and in preventing the loss of staff to the private sector.

Manpower training programmes may wish to use regional cooperation mechanisms (Technical Cooperation among Developing Countries (TCDC)), international fellowship programmes, attendance at scientific meetings in and outside the country, and training available at WHO collaborating centres.

2. Specific legal issues

Patents

Protection of intellectual property must be considered in developing a national drug policy. The issues are complex and cover all commercial and industrial activities. The appropriate agencies within the government should therefore work jointly in developing an overall policy for the country in relation to intellectual property.

Policies on brand and generic names

Since the 1950s, WHO has been responsible for assigning International Nonproprietary Names (INN) to pharmaceutical substances. These are generic names used for the easy identification of drugs.

Companies involved in research and development generally market their products under brand names (trademarks). In many countries, new pharmaceutical products are protected by a patent, brand name, or both for a fixed number of years. When the patent expires, the pharmaceutical product may become a commodity that competitors can produce and sell. The original company in most cases continues to sell the product, using the brand name originally adopted. New competitors may also give the product their own brand name. When one brand name is used for a product from multiple sources, the term “branded generic” is employed.

Pharmaceutical products may be offered for sale either under a specific brand name (trademark) or under the generic name. Multiple-source products may be put on the market either under a given brand name (branded generics) or under the generic name (commodity generic, INN) alone. A generic name is not the exclusive property of any individual person or corporate body. Brand names, on the other hand, are a form of commercial property. The question of brand names therefore has to be considered in the light of the country’s general policy regarding commercial property, a policy that will involve other commercial and industrial products in addition to pharmaceuticals. For this reason, in deciding national drug policy in relation to brand names, including such questions as permission to include the brand name on the label or what prominence it should have, consultation between the departments of health, trade, and industry and a review of the experience of other countries that have used alternative systems are advisable. Measures to regulate the use of brand names should take into account long-term national and social goals, including the need to encourage investment and research.

Prescribers may be allowed to prescribe by brand name or by generic name, specifying the manufacturer if two or more products are available for the same indications. Different countries, and different health institutions within them, use a variety of means to encourage prescribing and dispensing by generic names. A pharmaceutical product sold under its generic name is usually cheaper than its identical or equivalent branded product; prescription of generics can therefore result in significant monetary savings. In the purchase of drugs, however, whether or not potential savings are foreseen, the ability of the supplier to ensure continuous supplies of good quality is paramount. This may be especially important in countries where the regulatory agency is unable to ensure the quality of pharmaceutical products; there the cost of providing such assurance has to be weighed against the savings anticipated in the purchase of the least expensive products.

Generic substitution is practised in some health care systems where the dispensing of less expensive generic products may be optional or required. In such a case a constantly updated formulary of interchangeable generic drugs is needed.

3. Information and promotion

The Thirty-seventh World Health Assembly (1984), in resolution WHA37.33 on the rational use of drugs, *inter alia*, urged WHO Member States "to support the development and dissemination of unbiased and complete drug information". This was reiterated in resolution WHA39.27 (1986) which endorsed the WHO revised drug strategy. This strategy includes the establishment of ethical criteria for drug promotion based on the updating and extension of the criteria established in 1968 by the Twenty-first World Health Assembly in resolution WHA21.41. Ethical Criteria for Medicinal Drug Promotion, drafted by an International Group of Experts and reviewed by the WHO Executive Board *Ad Hoc* Committee on Drug Policies, were endorsed by the WHO Executive Board and will be submitted to the Forty-first World Health Assembly in May 1988.

Drug information

Information on and promotion of drugs may greatly influence their supply and use. Monitoring and control of both activities are essential parts of any national drug policy.

In addition to the information and promotional material provided by manufacturers, independent, reliable and objective information is also needed. This can be provided in the following ways:

- By the dissemination of independent scientific literature on the rational use of drugs and on therapeutic advances, as published by international organizations such as WHO, national regulatory authorities, and other scientific bodies.
- By a national drug information bulletin or newsletter. This is particularly helpful in some countries since it can outline the justification for important decisions taken by the local regulatory agency and can offer objectively written articles focusing on drug misuse and inappropriate prescribing practices.
- By national formularies, which can provide a comprehensive list of the pharmaceutical products, including dosage forms and strengths, available at the various levels of the health care system. The formularies can also be expanded to include prescribing and dispensing information and estimated costs of treatment.
- By the organization of training programmes, symposia, and lectures for the various groups of health personnel.
- By guidelines and educational material on the appropriate use of drugs by community health workers or paramedical personnel at the primary health care level.

— Through publications aimed at consumers and use of the mass media.

Any of these methods of providing information can be adapted to suit the needs and circumstances of individual countries.

Drug information sheets and labels

Provision of adequate drug information to consumers and prescribers and appropriate labelling are essential for the rational and safe use of pharmaceutical products. The drug information sheet or its equivalent and the label should be consistent with the information provided to the regulatory agency or its equivalent, and should be updated whenever significant new data become available and the necessary changes authorized. Both the manufacturer and the regulatory authority may propose changes. WHO provides draft drug information sheets for adaptation to local needs.

In countries with a low level of literacy, alternative ways of presenting information should be explored, particularly in relation to dosage.

In its second report (*7*), the WHO Expert Committee on the Use of Essential Drugs gave a sample list of the information that should be included in the drug information sheet. The list is intended for adaptation, as appropriate, to each country's needs. The sample list comprised the following:

(*1*) The international nonproprietary name (INN) of each active substance.

(*2*) Pharmacological data: a brief description of pharmacological effects and mechanism of action.

(*3*) Clinical information:

(*a*) Indications: whenever appropriate, simple diagnostic criteria should be provided.

(*b*) Dosage regimen (including route(s) of administration) and relevant pharmacokinetic data:
- average and range for adults, children, and the elderly;
- dosage interval;
- average duration of treatment;
- special conditions, e.g., renal, hepatic, cardiac, or nutritional insufficiencies, that require either increased or reduced dosage.

(*c*) Contraindications.

(*d*) Precautions and warnings (use in pregnancy, lactation, and other special circumstances).

(*e*) Adverse effects (quantified by category, if possible).

(*f*) Drug interactions (only if clinically relevant; interactions with drugs used for self-medication and with foods should be included).

(*g*) Overdosage:
— brief clinical description of symptoms;
— non-drug treatment and supportive therapy;
— specific antidotes.

(*4*) Pharmaceutical information:

(*a*) Dosage forms.

(*b*) Strength of dosage forms.

(*c*) Excipients.

(*d*) Storage conditions and shelf-life (expiry date).

(*e*) Package sizes.

(*f*) Description of the product and package.

(*g*) Legal category (narcotic or other controlled drug, prescription or nonprescription).

(*h*) Name and address of manufacturer(s) and importer(s).

Information on price may be added if desired.

The label should contain at least:
— the nonproprietary name (the brand name may be permitted in addition);
— the strength;
— the name and address of the manufacturer and importer;
— the storage conditions;
— the expiry date;
— the batch identification;
— the package size.

The price may also be included.

Both the drug information sheet and the label should be in the official language(s) of the country.

Whenever the drug product is dispensed in smaller quantitites than the package size of the manufacturer, it is necessary to decide what information is required on the label. As a general rule the consumer should be informed of the nonproprietary name of the drug (the brand name is optional). Other information may be included as follows:

— the patient's name;
— the strength;
— the prescriber's name;
— the manufacturer and importer;
— the dosage instructions;
— the expiry date;
— storage conditions;
— the batch identification – either the manufacturer's code or the pharmacist's prescription number;
— the indication (whenever appropriate).

Promotional activities

National drug policies should include provision for regulations dealing with drug information to ensure that health practitioners and professionals as well as consumers are provided with accurate scientific and other relevant data about drugs.

The ministry of health can have its greatest impact on drug information and promotion by defining, developing, and monitoring action to obtain a rational use of drugs and sound prescribing practices. Because new information is likely to become available with time, even in relation to existing products, there needs to be provision for official updating.

The regulatory agency should develop techniques for monitoring the dissemination of information. This information should deal with the safety of the drug, its approved uses and indications, the contraindications to its use, adverse reactions, the dosage, and other data.

The guiding principle is that the amount and type of promotional activity should be consistent with the terms and conditions of product approval. The methods of conveying drug information and the frequency with which it is conveyed will vary between countries, depending on commercial policy.

Consideration may also be given to control of the type and/or amount of resources expended on promotion. Such control may be exercised by the industry and the professions, or the government regulatory agency, or both.

4. Appropriate drug use

A policy aiming at the rational use of medicinal drugs needs to emphasize appropriate drug use if sound prescribing practices and the informed use of drugs by patients and public are to be achieved. Such a policy needs to address the problems of overprescription; inappropriate prescription; excessive self-medication; medication for transient ailments where there is no need for drugs; and use of new, expensive drugs when effective, safe, high quality drugs are available at lower cost.

A major contribution to the appropriate use of drugs can be made by the following actions:

(*1*) Educational programmes for health students can lay stress on pharmacological knowledge and good prescribing practice.

(*2*) Physicians, nurses, pharmacists and other dispensers of drugs should receive appropriate training.

(*3*) Data sheets, labelling and promotional material should be monitored by drug regulatory agencies for accuracy and validity.

(*4*) The pharmaceutical industry should make a commitment to provide accurate promotional material, for prescribers, dispensers and the public.

(*5*) Reporting on drug-related subjects by the mass media should be responsible and informative.

(*6*) Educational strategies and programmes on the appropriate use of drugs directed to the public should be developed and implemented.

As in all other aspects of a national drug policy, WHO acts as a facilitating and coordinating body through activities such as:

— publishing *WHO drug information*, and issuing newsletters with special attention to monitoring of adverse reactions to particular drugs and to stressing the need for comprehensive national health education and training programmes;

— preparing informational material on health care for the education of the public;

— assisting Member States in field research on drug prescribing (including physician self-auditing), drug consumption, drug performance, and patient compliance.

Further international collaboration is needed to launch research on appropriate dosages for vulnerable groups such as children, pregnant and lactating women, and the elderly, and to establish research programmes on drug assessment, with special emphasis on good prescribing practice.

5. Self-medication

Self-medication is widely practised in both developed and developing countries. For a variety of reasons it is desirable to encourage self-medication and every attempt should be made to ensure its appropriate use and to guard against any unacceptable risks it may entail. This juxtaposition of right and responsibility is expressed in the Declaration of Alma-Ata (*8*) which states that: "The people have the right and duty to participate individually and collectively in the planning and implementation of their health care. Governments have a responsibility for the health of their people which can be fulfilled only by the provision of adequate health and social measures."

The role of medicines for self-care can be summarized as follows:

- to provide quick and effective relief of symptoms that do not require medical consultation;
- to reduce the increasing pressure on medical services for the relief of minor symptoms, especially when resources and manpower are limited;
- to increase the availability of health care to populations living in rural or remote areas where access to medical advice may be difficult.

However, unrestricted availability in some countries of medicines for self-medication may result in their inappropriate use, delay in diagnosis, and waste of resources. Guidelines should therefore be developed and adopted to ensure that there is careful selection of drugs that are allowed to be sold without prescription for the short-term relief of symptoms when medical advice and accurate diagnosis are not required. A drug selection committee or an advisory review panel of experts representing professional, industrial and consumer interests can help in preparing such guidelines. Although the drugs authorized for self-medication will vary from one country to another – depending on the existing health care system, and social and economic factors – the criteria for selection are common for all and should be based on demonstrable efficacy, cost, and evidence of a wide margin of safety.

The drugs selected should be provided with standardized labels and instructions that are accurate and clearly understandable by lay persons. They should include complete directions on:

- indications for use;
- recommended dosages;
- warnings against unsafe use;
- warnings against drug interactions.

When feasible, there should be periodic review of the drugs authorized for over-the-counter sale and of labelling requirements, in the light of new information and experience.

Health education on appropriate self-medication should be organized through the media, and the medical and pharmaceutical professions. Since any drug carries some risk, the aim should be to provide objective information that will assist the consumer to judge the balance between potential therapeutic value and harm. Such educational programmes can also contribute to public understanding that medical advice should be sought when symptoms are not relieved by medication.

6. Health education

The purposes of health education are to enable people to improve their health and well-being, to ensure the most equitable and productive use of resources, and to encourage active public participation in defining and achieving health goals. It must be appreciated that "science and technology can contribute to the improvement of health standards *only* if the people themselves become full partners of the health care providers in safeguarding and promoting health" (*9*).

Appropriate health education is central to the safe and effective use of drugs and should begin at the earliest possible age. Schools and the home have an important role to play in this respect. Drugs cannot be used effectively if people are unwilling or unable to comply with drug regimens or if they think that drugs are safer or more effective than they actually are. Health education should accordingly be developed as an integral part of drug policy, and should involve individuals, the family, teachers, health professionals, the media, and government. It should include at least the elements listed below.

(1) *Education in the basic concepts of drug use*

It is important that people who use drugs understand, for example: the concept of the relationship between benefit and risk and how it is influenced by the nature and seriousness of illness; that the body eliminates drugs and that the speed with which this happens affects the frequency with which the drugs can be taken; that a drug can have effects on the body that are not intended; and that drugs do not retain their potency for ever (*10*).

(2) *Information about specific drug treatments*

If appropriate drug treatment is to become a reality, patients need to understand about the use, benefits, and limitations of the drugs they take. They need at least to know the name of the drug they are using; what the drug is intended to do and how to tell whether or not it is having the desired effect; how to recognize and what to do about possible adverse effects; and how to avoid or minimize problems by taking the drug in an appropriate way, including careful inspection prior to use to minimize the risk of taking the wrong medication.

(3) *Involvement in decision-making on drug policy*

Openness and effective communication are basic to the success of a drug policy. Public participation in the design and implementation of such a policy will foster the effective use and control of drugs.

Public participation is crucial to the attainment of health for all by the year 2000; it is needed to provide checks and balances in decisions relating to the allocation of resources and the acceptability of drug risks.

7. Monitoring and evaluation

A national drug policy can set goals but, whatever the state of development of a country, it can only be effective if it is properly implemented. To ensure success and to measure progress, the establishment of a peer group or of some other form of auditing system is recommended. Efforts should be made to set up a national evaluation scheme in which, *inter alia*, the national commitment can be measured by indicators such as changes in resource allocations, the accessibility and availability of drugs, and the increase in manpower in the pharmaceutical supply system.

Review of marketed drugs

The main reason for establishing a review system is to ensure that drugs of proven therapeutic value and quality are provided and properly used. It is advisable to carry out reviews at regular intervals, e.g., every five years, depending upon the resources available. Specific re-evaluations should be carried out as needed.

As a basis for regular review in an importing country, information is needed on indications, contraindications, side-effects, and the regulatory status of the drug in the exporting country. One way of ensuring regular review and updating of pharmaceutical products is for the competent authorities in importing countries to require recertification of imported products at regular intervals, e.g., every 3–5 years.

To limit the resource expenditure, groups of drugs selected for re-evaluation might be those used frequently, those with frequent side-effects, or fixed-ratio combination products. The re-evaluation should provide up-to-date information on standards of quality for the pharmaceutical product. Action against individual drugs might include changing quality standards or indications, warnings, restriction of use, or withdrawal from the market.

It is essential to inform the medical profession and the public of the results of the re-evaluation.

Post-marketing surveillance

Post-marketing surveillance is a mechanism for the systematic collection and analysis of data on how drug products are being used in the market and to what effect. Observations are made on safety, efficacy, and quality.

Monitoring of adverse drug reactions

It is recognized that the therapeutic trials that are adequate to justify registration of a drug for general use may fail to reveal uncommon adverse reactions. Hence there is a need to establish national monitoring systems for adverse reactions along the lines recommended in reports published by WHO (*11, 12*) and the Council for International Organizations of Medical Sciences (*13*). The cooperation of the medical and other health professions in this respect is important.

However, it may not be feasible for every country to establish a national monitoring system for adverse reactions. For this reason, and particularly in emergency situations when serious adverse reactions occur in one country and need to be communicated to other countries, a mechanism for rapid exchange of information between different national regulatory authorities is very important. The contacts established through the WHO International Drug Monitoring Scheme for adverse drug reactions and in the biennial Conference of International Drug Regulatory Authorities have greatly helped such exchange of information. If serious adverse reactions lead to withdrawal of a drug in one country the precise reasons and circumstances must be made known to others. This is because conditions vary with country and morbidity pattern so that a drug's withdrawal may be justified in one country and not in another. Each country should alert its health personnel to the need to report adverse reactions promptly to the regulatory authority.

The principal objectives of monitoring are to detect any adverse reactions, to minimize the time taken for their recognition, and to determine their relative overall importance in relation to the rational use of the pharmaceutical product.

The main activities of national centres for the monitoring of adverse drug reactions should include:

— The collection of data from such sources as voluntary reports from practising doctors, comprehensive monitoring in hospitals, and data on defined populations.

— Verification of data.

— The analysis of data. The quality of the results of the analysis will depend on the quality of the system for data storage and analysis.

— The support and promotion of comprehensive specialized monitoring centres and systems which can provide additional data, such as demographic data, and which may be especially useful for the investigation of drug safety problems.

It is desirable that validated data on adverse reactions should be made available to members of the health professions.

Monitored release

The data available on certain drugs intended for the treatment of specific diseases or appearing to have special advantages for some patients may not be sufficient to permit their release for general use. In such circumstances it may be desirable to release the drugs on a restricted basis, e.g., for use only in hospitals with special arrangements for monitoring patients.

Drug use

Information on drug use is essential for drug policy decisions. It may be used for the following purposes:

— to describe current patterns of drug usage (e.g., indications for which drugs are being used or the number of patients receiving the drugs for those or other indications);

— to determine changes in usage over time;

— to measure the effects on usage of education, information, regulation, and price;

— to define areas for further investigation into the efficacy and safety of drugs;

— to detect inappropriate use of drugs;

— to estimate drug needs in terms of morbidity patterns with a view to planning the selection, supply and distribution of drugs.

Convenient methods for establishing comparable drug statistics within and among countries have been developed by WHO (*14*). The classification system adopted is the Anatomical Therapeutic Chemical (ATC) Classification System, which is based on the same main principles as the International Marketing System Anatomical Classification System extended to include chemical groups and substances.

As a technical unit of measurement and comparison a "defined daily dose" (DDD) is used. Such units have been established for the most important drugs. When pharmaceutical product sales are expressed in terms of defined daily doses per unit of time and population, a rough estimate can be obtained of the number of patients being treated with a drug or group of drugs. Another advantage of using this unit of measurement is that it is independent of price and currency variations over time and among countries.

8. Financial resources

Many countries cannot afford or, for some reason, have not allocated the resources needed to purchase drugs to meet all their basic health care needs.

Ministries of health or analogous authorities need to justify, with meticulous care, all expenditure in the procurement and distribution of drugs. In addition to providing adequate data they must develop close ties and working arrangements with the national planning and finance authorities. These authorities in their turn need to appreciate the important contribution that the rational and economic supply and use of pharmaceutical products can make to national development goals.

The ministry of health can best achieve its goals by carefully estimating the total quantities of drugs needed and their cost. The assessment of needs should be prepared annually and, where appropriate, tenders should be called for at the time of the year when sufficient foreign exchange is most likely to be available. Failure to plan ahead in this way may mean that drugs have to be bought at greater expense on the local market and may lead to extra transport costs to prevent shortages and/or to meet emergency needs. If the tendering is competitive and the required foreign exchange is not subsequently made available, low-price suppliers may not be able to supply the drugs ordered; as a result, the country could become dependent on a single supplier charging high interest rates for late payment.

The highest priority in the allocation of limited foreign exchange should be for the supply of essential drugs. These drugs should be obtained at the lowest price consistent with good quality. Consideration must also be given to requirements for other products to meet critical medical needs.

9. Research and development

Research and development are essential features of national strategies for health for all by the year 2000, and the forms they might take and the processes and mechanisms for establishing priorities are much discussed within WHO Member States. An important component of such national health research strategies is drug research and development. Investment in this area can yield short-term and long-term benefits by leading to the development of badly needed new drugs, improvements in existing ones, and a more rational use of drugs.

The nature and scope of drug research and development obviously vary according to the health problems, interests and capacities of each country, and international health problems, challenges and opportunities. Drug research and development involve, *inter alia*, fundamental research in molecular biology and chemistry, immunology, and biotechnology, industrial research to convert scientific knowledge into useful technology, pharmacological and toxicological studies, and clinical and field trials of drugs and vaccines (with their related ethical considerations). Health systems research to measure the impact of national drug policies and accessibility to essential drugs is also needed, as well as health economic studies related to drugs, behavioural studies on prescribing problems at different levels of health care, the social and cultural aspects of drug use, self-medication, and utilization of services. As mentioned earlier, exploratory and developmental research into local raw materials and traditional medicines and evaluation of their use constitute another necessary area of research.

Of particular importance is the identification of research needs as a basis for deciding on research priorities. Such needs include new, more effective, less toxic, and more stable drugs and vaccines for existing conditions; drugs for "orphan diseases", i.e., diseases that affect relatively few people and for which the sale of drugs is therefore limited in quantity; and new drugs for newly emerging health problems, such as the acquired immunodeficiency syndrome. Information on drugs being developed in industrialized countries and relevant to the needs of developing countries should be made available to these countries.

Research is carried out by a variety of public and private bodies, among them the research-based pharmaceutical industry, universities, biomedical research institutes, and social and economic research institutes. Consumer associations might be encouraged to take part in studies on people's attitudes to prescribed drugs and self-medication, with a view to inculcating a more rational use of drugs.

There is inadequate information on the costs of drug research, and particularly of developing new drugs. It is certain, however, that research is expensive and fraught with uncertainty. Hence the cost factors involved in drug research and the methods of financing research have to be considered carefully before embarking on it.

Because of its very nature it is difficult to direct health research, and drug research is no exception. Nevertheless, research can be promoted and, to a certain extent, coordinated by a variety of means, including intellectual stimulation, scientific and technological competition, and financial incentives – whether private or public. Coordinating mechanisms vary in nature: some countries have medical or health research councils, some include health matters in more widely based scientific research councils, some have national institutes in which publicly funded health research is conducted, and some have private foundations whose selective investments in health research contribute to shaping priorities. The market intelligence systems of the research-based pharmaceutical industry also shape priorities. An important part of national drug policy is to draw the attention of all concerned in both the public and the private domains to the need for drug research that is relevant to the country's main health problems. At the international level, WHO is active in promoting drug research on the basis of sound information on health problems throughout the world. A national drug research policy should encourage the participation of the country's health research institutions and pharmaceutical industry, wherever they exist, in international drug research.

10. Technical cooperation between countries

To strengthen national and regional policies and to make the most of limited resources, technical cooperation is needed both between developed and developing countries and between developing countries themselves (TCDC). The following areas have proven suitable for such cooperation:

— evaluation of drugs;
— exchange of information;
— reporting of adverse drug reactions;
— quality assurance, and collaboration between regional and other quality control laboratories;
— WHO Certification Scheme on the Quality of Pharmaceutical Products Moving in International Commerce;
— pharmacopoeias and regional reference standards;
— inspection of pharmaceutical plants;
— transfer of technology;
— research and development;
— pooled procurement of drugs;
— training and manpower development;
— studies on drug classification and utilization;
— computerization of drug regulatory information;
— emergency situations.

The Association for South-East Asian Nations (ASEAN), the European Economic Community (EEC), the Nordic countries, and various groups of countries in the American Region provide examples of successful inter-country cooperation. Significant bilateral technical cooperation, of benefit particularly to developing countries, has taken place in the fields of technology transfer, establishment of drug quality control laboratories and distribution systems, and manpower training. For countries in the initial stages of development, international contacts and consultation can provide information and also help to avoid the repetition of errors committed elsewhere.

Such international contacts are of two types:

(*a*) between individuals working in similar areas; and

(*b*) participation in international programmes.

The contacts between individuals should be at more than one level in the organization. Not only should the head of the agency know and exchange information with counterparts in a number of countries[1] but corresponding contacts should be encouraged between the heads of such units as drug evaluation, laboratory services, and inspection and surveillance. These individuals should also make a point of learning of the organizational units in international agencies and institutions that can provide information on specific subjects.

The drug control agency, as opposed to individuals, should participate as fully as possible in international programmes of interest to the agency. Some programmes will of necessity be on a bilateral basis, others being sponsored at the international level by such agencies as WHO, e.g., the WHO International Conferences on Drug Regulating Authorities (ICDRA). Publications and newsletters such as *WHO drug information*, the monthly *Pharmaceutical newsletter* (which includes a list of addresses of individuals in regulatory agencies) and the *Essential drugs monitor*, provide information on drugs and on technical cooperation.

[1] See: *Proceedings of the 4th International Conference of Drug Regulatory Authorities, Tokyo, 6-11 July 1986* (co-sponsored by the Ministry of Health and Welfare of Japan and the World Health Organization).

References

1. JAYASURIYA, D. C. *Regulation of pharmaceuticals in developing countries: legal issues and approaches.* Geneva, World Health Organization, 1985.
2. WHO Technical Report Series, No. 645, 1980 (*WHO Expert Committee on Specifications for Pharmaceutical Preparations:* twenty-seventh report).
3. WHO Technical Report Series, No. 563, 1975 (*Guidelines for evaluation of drugs for use in man:* report of a WHO Scientific Group).
4. *International Nonproprietary Names (INN) for pharmaceutical substances: cumulative list no. 8.* Geneva, World Health Organization, 1988 (in press). Lists of proposed and recommended INN are issued periodically in the journal, *WHO drug information.*
5. *Official records of the World Health Organization*, No. 226, 1975, Annex 12.
6. WHO Technical Report Series, No. 704, 1984 (*WHO Expert Committee on Specifications for Pharmaceutical Preparations:* twenty-ninth report).
7. WHO Technical Report Series, No. 722, 1985 (*The use of essential drugs:* second report of the WHO Expert Committee).
8. *Primary health care. Report of the International Conference on Primary Health Care, Alma-Ata, USSR, 6-12 September 1978.* Geneva, World Health Organization, 1978 ("Health for All" Series, No. 1).
9. WHO Technical Report Series, No. 690, 1983 (*New approaches to health education in primary health care:* report of a WHO Expert Committee).
10. HERXHEIMER, A. & DAVIES, C. Drug information for patients: bringing together the messages from prescriber, pharmacist and manufacturer. *Journal of the Royal College of General Practitioners,* **32**: 93-97 (1982).
11. WHO Technical Report Series, No. 425, 1969 (*International drug monitoring: the role of the hospital:* report of a WHO meeting).
12. WHO Technical Report Series, No. 498, 1972 (*International drug monitoring: the role of national centres:* report of a WHO meeting).
13. COUNCIL FOR INTERNATIONAL ORGANIZATIONS OF MEDICAL SCIENCES. *Monitoring and assessment of adverse drug effects: report of a Working Group.* Geneva, CIOMS, 1986.
14. BERGMAN, U. ET AL., ed. *Studies in drug utilization: methods and applications.* Copenhagen, WHO Regional Office for Europe, 1979 (European Series, No. 8).

Suggested further reading

A new focus on pharmaceuticals. London, Pharmaceutical Economic Development Committee, 1986.

Policies for the production and marketing of essential drugs. Washington, DC, Pan American Sanitary Bureau, 1984 (Scientific Publication, No. 462).

National drug policies. Copenhagen, WHO Regional Office for Europe, 1979 (Public Health in Europe, No. 12).

MAMDANI, M. & WALKER, G. *Essential drugs and developing countries – a review and selected annotated bibliography.* London, Evaluation and Planning Centre for Health Care, 1985.

PATEL, S. J. *Pharmaceuticals and health in the Third World.* London, Pergamon Press, 1983.

* HELLING-BORDA, M. *The essential drugs concept and its implementation. Health in developing countries.* Unpublished WHO document, DAP 85/1.

* *Policies for essential drugs in primary health care – a course model.* Unpublished WHO document, DAP 85/3.

The rational use of drugs. Report of the Conference of Experts Nairobi, 25–29 November 1985. Geneva, World Health Organization, 1987.

Relevant resolutions of the World Health Assembly

WHA21.41, 1968.	Ethical and scientific criteria for pharmaceutical advertising
WHA23.45, 1970.	Pharmaceutical preparations
WHA24.56, 1971.	Prophylactic and therapeutic substances
WHA26.31, 1973.	Prophylactic, diagnostic and therapeutic substances
WHA28.65, 1975.	Prophylactic, diagnostic and therapeutic substances
WHA28.66, 1975.	Prophylactic, diagnostic and therapeutic substances
WHA31.32, 1978.	Action Programme on Essential Drugs
WHA31.33, 1978.	Medicinal plants
WHA31.34, 1978.	Organization of health systems based on primary health care
WHA32.41, 1979.	Action Programme on Essential Drugs
WHA35.27, 1982.	Action Programme on Essential Drugs
WHA37.32, 1984.	Action Programme on Essential Drugs and Vaccines
WHA37.33, 1984.	Rational use of drugs
WHA39.27, 1986.	The rational use of drugs

* Available on request from: Action Programme on Essential Drugs, World Health Organization, 1211 Geneva 27, Switzerland.

Annex 1

Working Group of Experts Geneva, 16-20 March 1987

List of participants

Members*

Dr A. A. S. Alwan, Chairman, National Board for Selection of Drugs, Ministry of Health; and Chairman, Department of Medicine, Mustansiriya College of Medicine, Al-Yarmouk, Baghdad, Iraq

Professor D. L. Azarnoff, D. L. Azarnoff Associates, Hillsborough, CA, USA

Mr R. A. Gosselin, President, Massachusetts College of Pharmacy and Allied Health Sciences, Boston, MA, USA (*Rapporteur*)

Dr B. Joldal, Director, Directorate of Health, Pharmaceutical Division, Oslo, Norway

Dr M. L. Lieberman, Director-General, Control of Health Resources, Ministry of Health, México, DF, Mexico

Dr J. Maneno, Deputy Director of Medical Services, Ministry of Health, Nairobi, Kenya (*Chairman*)

Mr C. Medawar, Social Audit Limited, London, England (*Rapporteur*)

Dr Pakdee Pothisiri, Deputy Secretary-General, Food and Drug Administration, Ministry of Public Health, Bangkok, Thailand

Dr D. Raditapole, Managing Director, Lesotho Dispensary Association, Mafeteng, Lesotho

Dr C. G. Roepnack, Bad Aibling, Federal Republic of Germany (*Vice-Chairman*)

Mr I. Saito, Director, First Evaluation and Registration Division, Pharmaceutical Affairs Bureau, Ministry of Health and Welfare, Tokyo, Japan

Mr M. Tan, Health Action Information Network (HAIN), Quezón City, Philippines

Secretariat

Mrs E. W. Dinius, Secretary, Action Programme on Essential Drugs, WHO, Geneva Switzerland

Miss S. Doyle, Administrative Assistant, Action Programme on Essential Drugs, WHO, Geneva, Switzerland

*Unable to attend: Professor N. Islaam, Director and Professor of Medicine, Institute of Postgraduate Medicine and Research, Dhaka, Bangladesh; Dr J. Svihovec, State Institute for Drug Control, Prague, Czechoslovakia.

Dr B. B. Gaitonde, Senior Public Health Administrator, Diagnostic, Therapeutic and Traditional Medicine, WHO Regional Office for South-East Asia, Delhi, India

Mrs M. Helling-Borda, Senior Scientist, Action Programme on Essential Drugs, WHO, Geneva, Switzerland (*Secretary*)

Dr E. Lauridsen, Programme Manager, Action Programme on Essential Drugs, WHO, Geneva, Switzerland

Annex 2

Meeting of Executive Board Ad Hoc Committee on Drug Policies, Geneva, 9-10 January 1988

List of participants

Members*

Dr R. Hapsara, Adviser to the Minister of Health, Ministry of Health, Jakarta, Indonesia (*Rapporteur*)

Dr A. P. Maruping, Director of Health Services, Ministry of Health, Maseru, Lesotho

Dr M. Quijano, Director, Department of International Affairs, Ministry of Health, México, DF, Mexico

Dr D. de Souza, Deputy Secretary and Chief Commonwealth Medical Officer, Department of Community Services and Health, Woden, ACT, Australia

Professor M. Steinbach, Director-General, Federal Ministry for Youth, Family Affairs, Women and Health, Bonn, Federal Republic of Germany

Dr K. Feiden, Head of Department, Federal Ministry for Youth, Family Affairs, Women and Health, Bonn, Federal Republic of Germany (*Adviser to Professor M. Steinbach*)

Professor B. Westerholm, Special Adviser, Ministry of Health and Social Affairs, Stockholm, Sweden (*Chairman*)

Dr F. E. Young, Commissioner of Food and Drug Administration, US Public Health Service, Department of Health and Human Services, Rockville, MD, USA

Mr N. A. Boyer, Director for Health and Transportation Programs, Bureau of International Organization Affairs, Department of State, Washington, DC, USA (*Adviser to Dr F. E. Young*)

Observers

Mr T. Kurokawa, Deputy Director, International Affairs Division, Minister's Secretariat, Ministry of Health and Welfare, Tokyo, Japan

Dr V. Reggi, Programme Manager, Essential Drugs Programme, UNICEF, New York, NY, USA

*Unable to attend: Dr. A. A. A. Nasher, Adviser, Ministry of Public Health, Aden, Democratic Yemen.

Dr T. Shimao, Chairman, Committee on Tuberculosis Control, Public Health Council, International Affairs Division, Ministry of Health and Welfare, Tokyo, Japan

Secretariat (WHO, Geneva, Switzerland)

Mrs P. Brudon-Jakobowicz, Scientist, Action Programme on Essential Drugs

Dr J. Cohen, Adviser on Health Policy

Miss S. Doyle, Administrative Assistant, Action Programme on Essential Drugs

Dr J. F. Dunne, Chief, Pharmaceuticals

Mrs M. Helling-Borda, Senior Scientist, Action Programme on Essential Drugs (*Secretary*)

Dr E. Lauridsen, Programme Manager, Action Programme on Essential Drugs

Dr A. Mechkovski, Senior Pharmaceutical Officer, Pharmaceuticals

Miss A. Wehrli, Senior Pharmaceutical Officer, Pharmaceuticals

Miss C.E. Whelan, Secretary, Action Programme on Essential Drugs

Also attending

Dr F.S. Antezana, Representative of PAHO/WHO, Guatemala, Guatemala

Ms S. Foster, Technical Officer, Action Programme on Essential Drugs, WHO, Geneva, Switzerland

Ms D. Fresle, Technical Officer, Action Programme on Essential Drugs, WHO, Geneva, Switzerland

Dr S.T. Han, Director, Programme Management, WHO Regional Office for the Western Pacific, Manila, Philippines

Dr I. Klinger, Adviser to the Regional Director, WHO Regional Office for the Americas/Pan American Sanitary Bureau, Washington, DC, USA

Dr H. Nakajima, Regional Director, WHO Regional Office for the Western Pacific, Manila, Philippines

Dr M. Ten Ham, Senior Scientist, Pharmaceuticals, WHO, Geneva, Switzerland

Dr G. Walker, Medical Officer, Action Programme on Essential Drugs, WHO, Geneva, Switzerland

Annex 3

Glossary of terms used in this report[1]

Term	Meaning	Source
Batch	A quantity of any drug produced during a given cycle of manufacture. The essence of a manufacturing batch is its homogeneity.	WHO Technical Report Series, No. 567, 1975, p. 17
Batch number	A designation (printed in numbers and/or letters on the label of a drug) that identifies the batch and that permits the production history of the batch, including all stages of manufacture and control, to be traced and reviewed.	WHO Technical Report Series, No. 567, 1975 p. 17 (adapted)
Benefit/risk ratio	The ratio of benefit to risk in the use of a drug; a means of expressing a judgement concerning the role of the drug in the practice of medicine, based on efficacy and safety data along with consideration of misuse potential, severity and prognosis of the disease, etc. The concept may be applied to a single drug or in comparisons between two or more drugs used for the same indication.	WHO Technical Report Series, No. 722, 1985 p. 49
Bioavailability	The rate and extent of absorption of a drug from a dosage form as determined by its concentration/time curve in the systemic circulation or by its excretion in urine.	WHO Technical Report Series, No. 722, 1985 p. 49
Compliance	Faithful adherence by the patient to the prescriber's instructions.	WHO Technical Report Series, No. 722, 1985 p. 49
Drug	Any substance in a pharmaceutical product that is used to modify or explore physiological systems or pathological states for the benefit of the recipient.	WHO Technical Report Series, No. 722, 1985 p. 49
Drug formulation	The composition of a dosage form, including the characteristics of its raw materials and the operations required to process it.	WHO Technical Report Series, No. 722, 1985 p. 49
Drug registration	The procedure of release of a drug for marketing after it has been evaluated by the competent health authorities.	International Federation of Pharmaceutical Manufacturers' Associations (IFPMA). Document IFPMA/75

[1] The definitions of terms given here are for the purposes of this report, and are not necessarily valid for other purposes.

Term	Meaning	Source
Drug utilization	The marketing, distribution, prescription and use of drugs, with special emphasis on the resulting medical, social, and economic consequences.	WHO Technical Report Series, No. 722, 1985 p. 49
Generic drug	Product marketed under a nonproprietary or approved name rather than a proprietary or brand name.	Executive Board, Seventy-third session, Geneva, 11-20 January 1984 (EB73/1984/REC/1 Annex 7, p. 60)
Generic substitution	The practice of substituting a product, whether marketed under a trade name or generic name, by an equivalent product, usually a cheaper one, containing the same active principle(s).	Executive Board, Seventy-third session, Geneva, 11-20 January 1984 (EB73/1984/REC/1 Annex 7, p. 60)
Efficacy	The ability of a drug to produce the purported effect as determined by scientific methods.	WHO Technical Report Series, No. 722, 1985 p. 50
Health needs	Scientifically (biologically, epidemiologically, etc.) determined deficiencies in health that call for preventive, curative and, eventually, control or eradication measures.	Official Records of the World Health Organization, No. 206, 1973, Annex 11, p. 103
Manufacturing	All operations involved in the production of a drug, including processing, compounding, formulating, filling, packaging, and labelling.	Official Records of the World Health Organization, No. 226, 1975, Annex 12, p. 88
Pharmaceutical product	A dosage form containing one or more drugs along with other substances included during the manufacturing process.	WHO Technical Report Series, No. 615, 1977 p. 35
Pharmacokinetics	The study of the rate of drug action, particularly with respect to: – the variation of drug concentrations in tissues with time – absorption, distribution, metabolism, and excretion of drugs and metabolites.	WHO Technical Report Series, No. 722, 1985 p. 50
Quality control	All measures designed to ensure the output of uniform batches of drugs that conform to established specifications of identity, strength, purity, and other characteristics.	WHO Technical Report Series, No. 567, 1975 p. 17
Therapeutic equivalence	Pharmaceutical products which, when administered to the same individuals in the same regimen, have essentially the same efficacy and/or toxicity.	WHO Technical Report Series, No. 722, 1985 p. 50